A FUN AND EASY WAY

Do Your Homework

Joy Berry

Illustrated by Bartholomew

Joy Berry Books
New York

Joy Berry Enterprises
146 West 29th St., Suite 11RW
New York, NY 10001

Cover Design & Art Direction: John Bellaud
Cover Illustration & Art Production: Geoff Glisson

Production Location: HX Printing, Guangzhou, China
Date of Production: July 2010
Cohort: Batch 1

Printed in China
ISBN 978-1-60577-320-9

When you need to do your homework and schoolwork, you need to know about:

- the purpose of schools
- ways of learning
- handling work you don't like
- getting your work done
- attitudes about homework

How do you feel when it is time to do homework or schoolwork? Do you sometimes feel frustrated and confused?

When you need to do your homework and schoolwork, do you wonder...

To understand the purpose of homework and schoolwork, it is important to understand the purpose of education. You go to school to learn the information and skills you need to survive and grow.

The purpose of homework and schoolwork is to help you learn what you need to know.

Some of what you learn is knowledge you acquire instantly.

You learned some of the things you know as soon as you experienced them.

For example, the first time you touched a hot stove, you learned immediately that touching a hot surface can be painful and dangerous. You didn't have to touch the hot stove again and again to learn this. Instead, you instantly acquired knowledge about what can happen when you touch hot things.

Some of what you learn is knowledge you acquire through repetition.

You learned some of the things you know by experiencing them again and again.

For example, if you are like most people, you didn't learn how to tie your shoelaces the first time someone showed you how. Instead, you had to try again and again before you learned to do it on your own. In other words, you learned by repetition to tie your shoes correctly and easily.

Your education should help you acquire both instant knowledge and knowledge through repetition.

To acquire knowledge instantly, it is often necessary for you to explore.

When you explore something, you try to learn about it by carefully investigating and examining it.

One way to explore is through observation. When you observe something, you look at it closely or watch it carefully.

Another way to explore is through experience. When you experience something, you use your five senses to interact with it directly.

Another way to explore is through research. When you research something, you gather information about it by talking to people, reading, watching TV, or listening to radio programs about it.

Still another way to explore is through experimentation. When you experiment with something, you use it and work with it to discover how it functions.

To acquire knowledge through repetition, it is often necessary for you to practice a set of skills. When you practice something, you do it again and again until you know it.

Sometimes it is necessary for you to memorize information. When you memorize something, you think about it again and again until you remember it.

To get the most out of school, you need to have opportunities for both instant knowledge and knowledge acquired by repetition.

Your learning experiences should involve
- observation
- experience
- research
- experimentation
- practice
- memorization

If any of these learning experiences are missing in the things you do at school, you might want to talk to your parents and teachers about it. Hopefully, they will find ways to include all of these experiences in your school program.

If you are like most people your age, you enjoy some learning activities more than you do others.

You might want to do the activities you like and avoid doing the activities you do not like.

Learning important information and skills sometimes requires doing things you do not enjoy.

When you are faced with activities you do not enjoy, avoid doing these things:

Avoid fooling yourself and others.

Do what you say you will do. If you tell yourself or someone else that you will do some work, keep your word!

If you do not keep your word, people will lose trust in you. Having others lose trust in you is not good, but not being able to trust yourself is worse.

Avoid procrastinating.

Complete the work you do not enjoy as soon as you can.

Once your work is done, you can do the things you enjoy doing.

Avoid escaping.

Do not try to get out of doing your schoolwork by doing any of these things:

Do not try to get out of doing your homework by doing any of these things:

To help yourself get your homework and schoolwork done, do the following things:

Do your homework as soon as you can after you get home from school.

If you do your work right away, you are less likely to forget to do it.

Finishing your work as early as possible frees up your time for other activities.

Make a game of doing your homework and schoolwork.

Set yourself a time limit for getting the work done. Be sure you give yourself enough time to do a good job.

See if you can complete your work within the time limit.

Reward yourself.

Promise yourself that you will do something you really want to do when your work is finished.

Be sure you keep the promise you make to yourself.

When your homework is finished, carefully put it away where you will remember to take it to school with you.
For example:

If you take a lunch box, book bag, or bike pack to school, put your homework in one of these places.

If you wear the same jacket or sweater every day, put your homework with the jacket or sweater.

You can also put your homework by the door so you will remember it as you leave for school.

Here are some wise sayings that can help you handle your homework and schoolwork:

Haste makes waste.

This means that hurrying too much might cause you to make mistakes.

If rushing to finish keeps you from doing a good job, you might end up having to spend extra time to correct your work.

Anything worth doing is worth doing right.

This means that if you are going to take the time to do something, you should do a good job.

If you are not willing to take the time to do something well, you should not do it at all.

Doing a bad job is a waste of time.

One step at a time.

This means that dividing a job into several steps can make it easier to do.

Do not try to work on everything at once. Do one step at a time, and this will make the job seem manageable and keep you from becoming overwhelmed.

First things first.

This means that you need to do work in order of its importance.

Do the most important work first.

This might mean that you need to do the more difficult or less enjoyable work before you do the easy things or the things you enjoy.

You might want to ask your parents or teacher to help you decide what order to follow in your work.

Sometimes there isn't enough time at school for you to finish all your work. When this happens, your teacher might ask you to do the work at home.

Schoolwork you do at home is called homework.

Different people have different opinions about homework.

The Argument in Favor of Homework

Some people think that homework is necessary if children are to learn everything that they are expected to learn. People who think this way believe that the things children learn at school must be practiced at home if they are to be learned well. These people also believe that homework is a good way to get children to learn to discipline themselves and be responsible for doing things on their own. People who believe this way think that homework is a necessary part of a child's education.

Argument Against Homework

Other people believe that children who have been in school all day need a break from schoolwork. These people point out that most adults are not expected to take their work home, so why should children? These adults also believe that what children do after school, the games they play, the friends they make, are very important and should not be interrupted by homework. They also think that homework can unnecessarily cause angry feelings between children and their parents.

If your teacher, your parents, and you do not agree about homework, it is important to discuss it together.

You might discover that your teacher, your parents and you disagree. If that is so, try to find a solution that will work for everybody.

If it is decided by both your teacher and your parents that you need to do homework, accept it and try to have a good attitude about doing it.

Doing your homework and schoolwork can help you learn the things you need and want to know, if you maintain a positive attitude about it and do the best job you can.